for Elise and Richie

CONTENTS

ABOUT THE AUTHOR

Iona May is a poet, performer and Religious Studies teacher based in Norwich. She writes about friendship, grief and what happens when societal expectations do not match personal needs. Her poems dwell on the beauty of human foibles, taking the trivial seriously and finding the ordinariness in catastrophe. She has presented a workshop about grief and clown-poetry at the Creative Bridges International Conference (2019). She also developed and showcased her poetry-show 'Red Jacket' through The Garage Theatre's competitive Scratch Night scheme.

Iona May
Breaking Down Loudly

VERVE
POETRY PRESS
BIRMINGHAM

PUBLISHED BY VERVE POETRY PRESS
https://vervepoetrypress.com
mail@vervepoetrypress.com

FIRST PUBLISHED SEP 2022

Printed and bound in the UK
by ImprintDigital, Exeter

ISBN: 978-1-913917-15-9

Cover image design: Rosey Priestman
(www.roseypriestman.com)

Acknowledgements

Breaking Down Loudly

Fool asks about my poetry

Why won't you turn to face our mum? I can't *Why won't you turn to face our mum?* I would make her flat *Why won't you turn to face our mum?* She is always changing *Why won't you turn to face our mum?* It's immoral to translate a person into words, it should only be encouraged in job applications because then everyone knows it's a lie *Why won't you turn to face our mum?* She is so broken I'd end up mending her beyond recognition *Why won't you turn to face our mum?* I wouldn't recognise her *Why won't you turn to face our mum?* She is so perfect I'd break her by accident *Why won't you turn to face our mum?* I won't put her on a pedestal *Why won't you turn to face our mum?* A child only looks at their mum if they don't trust her *Why won't you turn to face our mum?* I trust her *But she's dead.* She is too dead *So turn to face her.* Okay *What do you see?* She had brown hair.

Part 1

CREATIONS

The One-Woman Circus
One Night Only

Spotlight. All of a sudden, the Ringmaster is standing in it. She is the most awe-inspiring woman you have ever seen. She is about to speak. You are all anticipation, nothing else exists.

*

Greetings fine audience, watch closely as I

refract myself

        here I am and

                here I am

and I am my mother returning from her appointment   and I am

her eldest daughter just home for reading week

*

and there they both are! The eldest daughter stirs
risotto, feel how she loves the steam. The mother
comes in the back way, feel how she
hauls open their big blue gate. There is something
superhuman. And feel this – wait – the daughter
looks through the window and – now – sees her mum
feel that shift to familiar calm, that ground and how
reliably it holds. But look up. A sentence is falling

*

Sentence piercing earth's atmosphere

Mother passing bike shed

Sentence reaching maximum velocity

Mother passing apple tree

Sentence falling through rain clouds

Mother passing only-spikes rose bush

Sentence startling pigeons

Mother stepping uneven steps

Sentence falling through brickwork

Mother on the threshold to kitchen

Sentence falling through doorframe

Mother opening her mouth

Sentence landing on her tongue

Mother looking at her eldest daughter

it's cancer and there's a lot of it

*

swallow

feel swallowed, dragged downwards
look up now – a bright picture-book heart turned dot

gone   and this is how it is

when words coagulate

right here in my mother's gullet, you want to be
tangible. This tightening relaxing, this warm pulse,
desperate to shed that lonely
timelessness and
gurgle and brush up against and oh to be
a million times encased,
aching, squishy and there is

something
about this body. Something generous maybe.
Or possessive. Or something that is also

so desperate to hold something. Or it could just be very random chance

that now

here I am. In her small intestine. Solid.

*

Everything has to solidify eventually.

I'm looking at you. Translucent
Eldest Daughter. What will you be?

You've eaten risotto and left and come back
until you know the train-line to Lancaster

like a lullaby, you have tried to understand
salvation and emptiness and

how to express
your own secret longings. Or not.

How bad-ass is Draupadi? or Kadijah?
or Mary? or modern-day witchcraft? What a

fascinating degree, opens so many doors
its draughty. Did you hear about

what happened to the eldest daughter
who was made out of open doors?

Of course not.
She was invisible. So let me help you

find yourself
a real body – here

take my red jacket, take these shiny
black shoes. Let them hold you

upright, plant your feet on new ground
see how they become you and yes

how suave you are, how dynamic, alive, inspiring,
vivid and yes, as if by magic, there you are –

A Secondary School Philosophy Teacher!

*

Okay then Year Seven, we're putting it to a vote –

if you belonged to the place of
ice cream that never unexpectedly
plonked on sand and

mum swam way out with you
then back again to once-dot towels
forever sun-warmed-ready

dad shared out an apple
like he'd trained for years
one slice for you one for

sister who was bold enough
to play with the waves but
scared enough to make you brave

and you got the chance
to break right out of there
then would you?

(and, discerning audience,
doesn't that gorgeous red jacket make me
such a great teacher?!)

*

Cancer in the dark. Sea anemone. Supernova.
Makes you think: Vast. Can't get enough

existence – so easy once you're used to it. *Watch me
duplicate*. Tendrils bright with newness reach out –
their first-time touching, best ever feeling, such
sweet warmth. Nestle in so cosy so connected so

desperate to duplicate. *Kind arteries please
hug me, I'm hungry*. Existence knows nothing
but dependence. *I'm not needy, I need.* Existence
so moreish once you're hooked on it. What a
generous intestine, keeps on giving. *Tell me how.*
Digestion, it's complicated. Simpler to
duplicate. *What am I?* Existence disorientates
if you over think it, too much trying

to fit in, too claggy, too much swelling and
thinning. Too much can't get enough. *I'm bored
of myself. Can't duplicate*. This wearisome
weightiness, blocked up wanting, exhaustingly
anxious and clumsy existence. *Gentle muscles

I'm hungry, let me absorb you* This useless
intestine, doesn't know anything. What happened
to that homey-ness. *Please someone tell me

what am I for?* Lonely bones like doorframes
without walls. *I'm cold*. Existence flickering

in the vastness. So beautiful, truly it is

*

Okay then Year Ten, who can tell me the answer

to this real-life example of The Problem
Of Personal Identity: If the cancered woman no longer has the fat
I snuggle against then is she still my mum?

*

So now we've almost arrived at the true origin of things, right here –

our apple tree, lit up by morning. Our roses,
a memory of sunrise. Our confident house, come in!
Curtain-muffled light. Everything outline. It's too quiet
for the rustle of your popcorn. So hush. And here

I am – my little sister, sleeping. It's unusual
to see her so unanimated but, still, her tug at our
centre, reaching out to protect to compete to
protect to. Still, she is too beautiful. And here

I am – my father's voice on the phone. His tone
echoes with tiredness but, still, reminds us of
easy untangling. Still, he is too heroic. Yes, hush
so we can only hear breathing, and watch me

create!

*

Sally

......

Sally

......

Wake up Sally

I'm awake!

Dad's on the phone

Dad? On the phone?

He's at the hospice

......

He wants to speak to you

......

Sally?

What is it?

He wants to speak to you

Why?

......

                                        I'm sleeping

Come on

                                                    ......

......

                                        Can't he just tell it to you

......

                                        I'm sleeping

He told it to me already

                        So tell it to me when I'm done sleeping

Just take the phone okay.

The Ringmaster turns to face all of you in the audience.

She can't dodge my Big Bang forever

KABOOM!

Mum's death falling backwards and forwards through spacetime so

Now her death falls when she is admitted to the hospice
Now her death falls when her radiotherapy doesn't work
Now her death falls when the surgeons cut her open but can't remove anything
Now her death falls when her GP shows her the scans
Now her death falls when she stops having the energy to go swimming
Now her death falls when her mum's young death teaches her to do the same
Now her death falls when her premature birth teaches her she doesn't deserve too much aliveness

Mum's death falling backwards and forwards through spacetime so

Now her death falls when her body is buried

Now her death falls when her family go to Sri Lanka for Christmas without her

Now her death falls when she cannot tell her eldest daughter the risks of quitting her teaching job

Now her death falls when her kitchen is redecorated

Now her death falls when her eldest daughter gives birth and she cannot be grandma

Now her death falls when she cannot congratulate her eldest daughter for winning the T.S. Eliot Prize

Now her death falls when her eldest daughter dies

KABOOM!

*

Thankyou thankyou thankyou. Oh what a jaw dropping start to the night! I was on the edge of my seat, spellbound. And that gentleman over there was crying, yes you Sir, don't pretend I didn't catch you – just a little tear maybe? just a trickle? No? He was distraught everyone, that's right kids– a grown man! Be proud of yourself Sir, I wanted to cry too. Lucky for you, I hold back my tears – wouldn't want to have to issue a flood warning! Tears of misery, tears of laughter, that terrible sense of unease, gasps of wonder, breath-taking stillness – it's a rollercoaster tonight and we've got plenty more drops and twists ahead – these death-defying stunts are not for the faint hearted, don't stay if you can't handle it! No but honestly folks, it's a joy and a delight you all came out tonight, none of this would be possible without you. Each and every one of you is unbelievably fantastic! I want you to give YOURSELVES a huge round of applause. I can't hear you! Com'on let's see if we can wake up the old folks out in Cromer. THAT'S MORE LIKE IT! And so – without further ado – let me introduce my fantabulous performers, keep up your hearty clapping forrrrrrr

Myy sister! Oh the way she dances! Empty space
suddenly sensuous, switching places with her
hips, wrists, shoulders, feet, and all of this

joy, where does it come from? Actual joy
none of that fake stuff to make smile-lines ache, no no

the genuine unfurling of it. How does she manage

to be all the way up there
sequined, summersaulting, and – at the same time –
stomping about? any of us could join her

we already know which floorboards creak,
how to be so sorry not sorry for the neighbours

Give me another round of applause then for the Dancing-Joy-Makerrr! AKA

Sally   Sister   Little Sister   The Best Person In The World

The Most Annoying Person In The World

A spotlight please forrrrrr

The Juggling Extraordinaire! How many things can he keep up in the air?

bunch of flowers   hoover

his daughter   her a-level stress   saucepan

special moment for the family   dustpan

and brush   soft boiled egg

the odds of recovery

another daughter   her teaching stress   special moment with his wife

a-hundred-and-one emails   a cacophony of do-gooders

correct painkillers   tupperware

butter dish

oops! What a crash!

and – in a puff of smoke – his poise vanishes. *NOOOOOOOOOOOOOOO!*
MY FAVOURITE BUTTER DISH IN THE WHOLE WORLD!

My juggling dad everyone, AKA

Sensitive Man   Roguish Man   Loving Husband

Too-Many-Balls-In-The-Air-Butter-Dish-Breakerrrrrrrrrrr!

Even louder forrrrr

My dying star / almost black hole   of a mother   can you feel

the pull of it?   her intensifying gravity   like she's becoming

everyone's most exquisite crush   so captivating you don't even

notice furniture or walls or whatever's through the window   but

only that gauntness   gives her a certain   vivacity

those big brown eyes   so tragic   so wise   that surely she

already sees beyond all of this   her skin so tender   she must

sense those in-between emptinesses   don't you wish you could

breath more quietly   because when there is an absolute

moment she will tell you something spectacular   listen close

I miss my true body   I want to be fat again   it's weird

how she puts you at ease when it's so obvious her smile is a trick

I guess some women would die for a thin body like this   mum

can't you be more like a fucking star?   too inanimate to grieve

Yes folks, now able to fit into a leotard, it's my all-too-human mum, AKA

Cancered Woman   Strong Brave Woman

Lovingly Rememberrrrrrrrrrred

And – last but certainly not least – it's the woman you've all come out for, is she generous or exploitative? real or dishonest? dangerous or fragile? No one will ever know. But she's sure bringing you one hell of a show tonight. You can see it but will you believe it? Hands together now forrrrr myyyyyyy Self!

Her amazing her tantalising
cycling to school and crying! How did she
dodge that bus? Practically impossible
when tears turn traffic to rainbows.

Don't try it at home kids
if you ride downhill you should
use your brakes, wear a helmet,
not be so terribly sad.

There is massive risk her particles,
indifferent to each other, will drift
skywards. Marvel at the strength
she has to hold them all together.

And now look – she's powering up
the steepest hill ever! The miracle
of this body! actual legs! actual feet!
in actual worn-down shoes!

And this, everyone, is the only place I ever cry. That's right grand
audience, it's the one and only Dare-Devil-Poet! AKA

Iona   Eldest Daughter   Philosophy Teacher   Ringmaster

Trickster   Fool   Clown

Part 2

THE
MEMORIAL
WOODLAND

The Memorial Woodland

The funeral director shows us the piece of ground that our
mum will be buried beneath. Clown applauds. Fool asks why

we're making a fuss when everyone dies. *Your mother had a
beautiful name,* the funeral director says, *d'you know it means hope?*

My daughter's name too. Trickster makes plans to exchange
the funeral director's hope for our hope. Fool asks why

no one is saying this is sad. The funeral director says, *my daughter
loves horses*. Trickster decides to trip up the daughter's horse

when she's out riding. The funeral director says, *your mother's
special burial plot costs £745.* Clown empties her pockets so

washingmachine tissue-snow goes everywhere. Then takes
a credit-card from her shoe. Trickster tells the funeral director

our mum was a pornstar so we've got plenty of cash. Fool asks
how much it costs to make the dead stay dead. Trickster shows

the funeral director a picture of our mum sunbathing topless
and saggy. She tells him his wife can't compare. Clown explains

we could never have enough to show how grateful we are so she'll
become a gravedigger to make up the short-fall. She can't help smiling

as she shows off her digging. The funeral director says, *it's so
sad but your mother will live on in your hearts.* Fool asks why

it is sad. Trickster eats the funeral director's tie and tells him it
lives on in his heart. Clown puts her eyes to our chests to check if

our mum's there. The funeral director hands us a pen to make note
of additional costs. Trickster finds his tie in the pen-lid. Fool asks

if ties generally prefer to get cremated or buried. Clown informs us
it's night in our chests. The funeral director says, *what about flowers?*

Mum, without you, I'm the only one

wanting the ritual of lunch. Dad & Sally
just grab bread & cheese whenever. So I'm alone
at our table again, pretending to be all blasé

Listen to this –

I'm applying for a Teaching Assistant job
writing, 'I will quietly break down information
into manageable chunks'. It conjures my mum
and she's laughing at me, *this could read like
you'll quietly break down into tears.* We're both
laughing, *yes employ me! I am highly qualified
in quietly breaking down!* When did writing
become such a warm meeting place?
She used to tell me, your sentences
do not make sense. I'd tell her, *your perfectionist
will haunt me forever, I will never forgive you.*
Now, oh this dreaming into plausible lies, oh this
straying to absurdity. *But is it too true mum?
When you were so sick, when you were just dead
was I breaking down? But so quietly because
who had time for the fuss? Maybe I was
fine but* it's too true of her body, quietly
breaking down while she focused on work
too much to hear it and she tells me, *I blame
my perfectionist for my cancer, held-back
feelings trapped in my gut.*

From Jacket

I understood the contours of your shoulders
they were so brave they wanted to
fold inwards to protect that soft place at your centre
because there is too much
clamorous light out there for a body
losing her mother in a classroom where
teenagers are so disgustingly alive
with the jabber of their insecure edges
your shoulders were iron enough
like armour not fragile like wings but scared of
appearing too small with bad posture
in a classroom where you thought they should
be intimidating I was there with my shoulder pads
so together we opened but did not
expose because I gently hugged the ache of you
my red was for *keep out danger of death* and
I was loose to make your breasts unimportant
but could feel them within me close
then receding with your ribcage
with your lungs with the need for air
your heart *still here still here still here* and
the pace of it was the panic of you until
together we steadied then this was a classroom
where we conducted their insights
and the way your arms moved was so
exhilarating but we don't do that anymore
you don't need me like you used to

Journaled response

I am crying and crying and dad said he doesn't care if I'm upset because I can't teach and I'm such a broken stupid unassertive human being and I was crying and crying and dad said 'I don't care about you whatever you do I know you'll be fine' and I was crying and he said 'I don't care' and I hate him so much

Clowned response

Mum Clown and Dad Clown stand shoulder to shoulder centre stage. Dad Clown is holding a folded blue piece of material like it's a baby. They are both looking at it then looking at each of you in the audience and everyone is in love with the blue piece of material.

Dad Clown: Our wonderful daughter

Mum Clown: Do you think she'll be alright?

Dad Clown: Nothing in the world will harm her

Mum Clown: But she's very blue

Dad Clown: My favourite colour!

Mum Clown: What about scissors or plug sockets? It's a painful
world out there if you're blue

Dad Clown: [*singing*] Blue is the colour, our daughter is so strong, we're all together and our daughter is so strong!

Mum Clown looks at Dad Clown then takes a corner of the material and pulls at it. She moves away from Dad Clown while holding the material until eventually it unravels into a blue square hanging between the Clown Parents. It catches the sunlight from a nearby window. The Clown Parents look at it and look at each other and look at each of you in the audience and it is the most beautiful thing anyone has ever seen.

Mum Clown: Wow

Dad Clown: Wow

Mum Clown: Nothing can harm her! [*singing to the blue material*] Blue is the colour I don't care about youuuuuuu, blue is the colour whatever you do I don't care about youuuuuuuuu

Dad Clown joins in and as they sing they flutter the material so it is the sea, the sky, a waterfall, a windy day etc. The singing becomes faster and the Clown Parents become less interested in the material and more interested in each other. Finally, they joyously throw the material into the air and it lands in a heap on the floor.

Mum and Dad Clown: [*singing*] I don't care about you blue no whatever you do blue I don't care about you etc.

They are singing and dancing and looking at each other and looking at each of you in the audience and everyone is so happy.

Mum and Dad Clown exit, dancing fast-waltz style.
Blue Material alone where it fell centre stage.

Also at the Memorial Woodland

The funeral director led Dad, Sally, and I from one place to another. We passed a huge rectangular pond with giant goldfish in it. Dad asked what the goldfish liked to eat and the funeral director replied anything rich in protein.   On the car journey home, I told them that the funeral director probably fed dead bodies to the fish. Dad laughed but Sally didn't.   I wanted to write about Clown, Fool and Trickster feeding the fish but those three are better framed by an ordinary world. I wrote about the burial plot instead, even though mum actually bought it before she died.   We were eating spaghetti when she told us. I said oh that's nice like she was a child who'd said she'd bought a spaceship.

One month after mum's death, Sally gets all A*s

I hear the word star and become one – my whole body
stretched to a five pointer. It's been so long since I exposed my centre, it feels
ok actually, not as bad as I thought, quite nice even and I say *Sally, I'm here
and I'm wide open to hug.* But I can't work out if she wants
me and my arms are aching

Dinner party

dad is the centre person I HATE HIM he hovers

his hand above his chest when he talks HATE HIM like he's pulling words

from his heart up his throat out his mouth DISGUSTING so precise

so earnest DISGUSTING no one here knows him HATE THEM only knew

husband&wife I TOOK IT FOR GRANTED dad was

the edges person LOVED HIM rock by the dresser that introverts

eddied around LOVED HIM mum laughed loudly GRANTED conducting

them all TOOK HER FOR GRANTED each person here is a husband&wife

HATE THEM dad and I can't bring ourselves to disassemble

this knife with fork wineglass-set room HATE HIM prompt each other

to talk about our successes DISGUSTING *Iona's*

teaching year seven drama this year THEY LOVE US *dad's got a great*

new website for his sensory-motor-psychotherapy LOVE US *we went to*

mum's grave yesterday LOVE US *planted an apple tree*

Instructions

You are about to draw a map
of your family history.

Take one piece of lined A4 paper,
keep it portrait.

The vertical space on the paper is time –
the top is when your parents first met, the bottom is now.

So write your mum's name and your dad's name
far apart at the top of the paper.

The horizontal space between the names is the emotional
closeness or distance between the people named.

Move to the next line down, remember
this shows that time has passed.

On this new line, write your mum's name and dad's name again.
Will you place them closer now they have spent time together?

On the next line, write their names again
and so on.

When your mum gives birth, start to include
the name of her child on your map.

Don't panic when you have more than two people on your map. It is almost
possible to show ALL of their emotional closenesses or distances.

When your mum gets cancer, find a way
to represent this.

A Family History

Mum

Dad

Dad

Mum

Mum Dad

MumIona Dad

Dad   Iona Mum

Mum

Iona Dad

Dad Mum   Iona

Iona Dad

MumSally

Mum Sally   Dad Iona

Dad Mum Sally Iona

Mum Dad   Iona Sally

Dad Mum   Sally   Iona

Sally

Mumum Dad

Iona

Dad Sally

Mumumumumum

Iona   Sally Dad

Dad

Iona Mumumumumum Sally

Sally Iona

Dad Mumumumumum

Iona Sally   Mummumumumumumumumum   Dad

mumumurum Sally mumumumum Dad mumumumum Iona mumumumum

mum

Iona Dad Sally

Sally   Dad   Iona

Dad Sally

Iona

Mumumum Iona

Dad

Sally

Iona

Christmas leftovers

Mum's sanitary towels outlived her
but they are all gone now I really need one

I am so proud of our Christmas Tree

Sally brings olives and wine and baklava
How can she even do that and be the little sister?

What's it like for Dad? Suddenly
hair-ties are everywhere

I am so proud of all our mugs on hooks

Tube station charades
is the best game and we invented it

Me to Sally: no you see your introduction isn't just your map
it's also your compass

Dad bought Sally a bowl for Christmas, he is so pleased
but it is a bowl

Mum's last ever sanitary towel has a fifty-pound note hidden inside

Never the less
we all laugh about essay-only words

Dad to Sally: I'm not disappointed in you I'm disappointed
in Netflix for keeping you away in your bedroom

Further more over

Sally to Me: you eat so much

Elephant and Castle is too easy

To atone for Netflix we sit in the sitting-room together to watch a real film
a turtle turns into a woman for a man alone on an island

On the other hand where is the other hand?

I catwalk my Christmas slippers round the kitchen
Should've got Sally something extra

Journaled response

To Everyone. You have no idea – mum is collapsed in agony on her way from bath to bed. She is naked on the landing floor, all spine and screaming and I actually do not know what it looks like. She always says *don't look* so I don't. I just walked around her on my way upstairs. You have no idea – how easy that is. Soon I'll hear her screaming again and just fall asleep right away. You have no idea – some things are so regular I can't explain them clearly. Like brushing my teeth. Actually, probably mum is screaming while I am brushing my teeth most evenings. So ordinary. But I can never just mention it. You have no idea – how lonely this is. The way you'd go all hush and big-eyed.

Clowned response

Mum Clown and Daughter Clown enter. Mum Clown takes big confident steps, Daughter Clown walks just behind her. Mum Clown stops at the centre of the stage. Daughter Clown stops next to her. Mum Clown looks at each of you in the audience and everyone is delighted by how much she enjoys being looked at. Daughter Clown looks at Mum Clown and then looks at each of you in the audience and everyone is relieved by how baffled she is by Mum Clown's confidence.

Mum Clown: We are here to tell you about my pain

Daughter Clown: Yes, we are here to tell you about her pain

Mum Clown and Daughter Clown look at each other. They are clearly unsure what to do next. They look at each of you in the audience – it's a moment of the pretending-to-know-everything game, then

Mum Clown: [*full of joy*] We will give you a demonstration

Daughter Clown: Yes, here is a precise demonstration of my mum's pain

Daughter Clown starts to hum. She lifts her hands above her head and the pitch of her humming gets higher then – with a small jazz-hand wave – she brings them down near her waist. As she does this the pitch of her humming gets lower. She continues like this and Mum Clown joins in.

Mum Clown tries to copy her exactly, but Mum Clown's movements are bigger and less precise. Mum Clown's hands keep finding themselves high in the air when Daughter Clown's are lower down and visa-versa. Finally, Mum Clown gives up and shimmies her whole self to the ground.

Daughter Clown looks at her, stops humming and lets her arms fall to her side.

Mum Clown: Aaaaaaaaaaaaaaaaaaaaaaaaaaaaaaaahhhhhhheeeeeeeeeeeeeeeee
eeeeeeeeeeeeeeeeoooooooooooooooooooooooowwwwwww
weeeeeeeeeeeaaaaaaaaaaaaaaaahhhhhhhhhhhh

Mum Clown looks at Daughter Clown and looks at each of you in the audience and everyone is delighted by how much she enjoys being looked at.

Daughter Clown looks at Mum Clown and looks at each of you in the audience and everyone is relieved by how baffled she is by Mum Clown's behaviour.

Daughter Clown: What happened to our humming routine?

Mum Clown: [*still lying on the floor*] Oh I just got too distracted by being in pain [*rolling and kicking her legs in the air*] Aaaaaaaaaaaaaaaahhhhhhhhhhhha
aaaaaaaaaaaaaaaaaaaaaaaaaaaaaaaahhhhhhhhhhhhhhhhhhhhh
eeeeeeeeeeee

Daughter clown watches her, baffled.

Daughter Clown: [*to audience*] I'm so sorry

Mum Clown: [*standing up and wiggling her hips*] oooooowwwwwwwaaaaaa
    aaaaaaaaaaaaahhhhhhgony aaaagaaaggaaaaaaaagggoneyyyyyyy

Daughter Clown: [*serious tone. Playing the pretending-to-be-in-control game*]
    There it is everyone! A precise demonstration of my mum's pain

Daughter Clown waves her jazz-hands towards Mum Clown with a hummed ta-da.

Mum Clown: owwwwwww [*pirouetting*] ittttttttsssssaaaaaaaaaaaaaaaaaaaagggg
    gggggguuuuuuunnnnneeeeeee eeeeeeeeeeeeeeeeeey! Suchaaaaaaa
    aaaaaaaaaaaaaaaaaaaaaaaaaaaaaaaaaaaaaagggonnnneeeeyaaaaaa
    aaaaaaaaaaaaaaahhhhhhhhh

Mum Clown and Daughter Clown bow.

They walk towards the exit together, talking about their show.

Mum Clown: I hope you didn't mind that I took the lime-light

Daughter Clown: Really, pain demonstrations should be much more
    civilised.

Empty Tupperware

all those friends with all their hope

she's eaten it

oh please dear sweet something

flesh her out

built from twigs

she is so hungry and so alive

and i am so alone

washing up and putting away and putting away and i can't

fit the tupperware in the cupboard

tumbling all over everything all over everywhere

what is the point?

What you do for mum's last Christmas

You wash up and tell your sister
she's spending the whole time
sorting out the soundtrack
rather than actually
clearing the table
she says I am helping
puts on The Contours
Do You Love Me?
years later it'll be your
christmas song but right now
there are four places to clear
and you are dancing
with your bum only
so you can still scrub the plates
your sister dancing the dirty
pans towards you dancing
her whole body
she is the best in the world
you are ready for the moment
to turn *like-a mashed-potata*
both jumping so water flicks
and your hair everywhere
now *do-the twist* you are
miming a superstar
she is jiving her hips

Ideal state

*'We won't allow them to imitate a woman
young or old, whether she is ... boasting of
her supposed happiness, or overwhelmed
by misfortune, grief and tears.'*
(Plato: *The Republic*)

Remembering I have a body I realise
it aches to be touched, I can't touch
my toes, stretching makes me sad, don't cry
just want to. I'm told that these days
you can only see grieving women
on the internet. Your screen fills
with the collapse of it – saliva and snot
even with cameras watching, screams
splintering roots into sky all mouth
and shuddering. I could never.
Show me how. I'm scared that
after my friends have each died
in their own particular ways, I'll still
just be sat here thinking I really
should be bothered to take up yoga

A teacher's guide to loudly breaking down

SHOUT THE CAPITALS

Eat all the cake in the staffroom

    CAKES MAKE MY MUM SCREAM AND SHIT

    WHAT IS MY MUM?

Get some red paint and vandalise the desks then walls

    THIS RED IS HER CANCER

    WHAT IS MY MUM?

Vandalise their schoolwork

    THIS RED IS THE ONLY TRUE THING

    WHAT IS MY MUM?

Carry a huge dog-basket and throw yourself into it mid-lesson

    I'M TOO BORED

    WHAT IS MY MUM?

Hurl all of the chairs through all of the windows

    MAKING A MIRROR OF MY SHATTERING

    WHAT IS MY MUM?

Face all their faces with the full glaring of your hollowness

FUCKING LOOK AT ME

WHAT IS MY MUM?

Leap out a smashed-up window and stomp to the shore

SEA! GIVE ME A NEW MOTHER

WHAT IS MY MUM?

Noise like a sea-lion

DONT DARE TELL ME HOW TO BE

Part 3

BREAK RIGHT OUT OF THERE

from all the way in bristol dad's new girlfriend texts   **this shift**

must seem weird for you   is she asking if i hate her   do i   i haven't

left norfolk since christmas   it is true

about the sky here   it is too subtle   how is it possible to exist

in so many different places simultaneously   i message christina and

she is so close and   in london and in my memories

of that redland houseshare   the whole world

grief heavy afresh frying broccoli   lets risk it

and go to porto for easter   the sky is so full

with white light i can't bear it   or lets hold off booking

till the weekend   i am vanishing or

actually gradually dispersing   there are so many people

to listen out for   elise's voice in french in the hallway

and by the stream at the end of her dad's garden   in the kitchen she

pours us wine in english   how was work   is your sister

still annoying   shall we try to make our own

prayer flags on dead-mother's day   i don't hate

my dad's new girlfriend but   we think on the same frequency

it could be difficult   i should move back to bristol

probably   mum couldn't have imagined me

all the way over here   she went off-grid first though so

can't know elise or christina or any of my favourites   i feel

so tenderly the morning sky   though the crack i left for it   everyone

Lockdown house-share

Let's all do exercise together in the garden. 10.30? I am trying get up but keep dreaming. Or not? No one has to if they don't want to. I can't work out if I love it or lump it that you all know when I am sad before I do. It's not a big thing though just a small thing just that I sent voice recordings telling the last week of Jesus's life to Ethan and to Prerna and I was so pleased with myself and it's actually embarrassing and oh oh I'm waiting to see what they say it's such a big thing for me and now you all know it's nothing to worry about. By the way, I can tell if you're happy or sad from the music you play. Even though it's same songs always. Maybe you absorb more sound when you're feeling like you don't know what to do with yourself. We could run an experiment but I don't have the inclination. Too busy learning to read novels again. So aware of holding the book that I rarely make it to Italy. 'My Brilliant Friend'. I will be forever altered by my new softness towards all of you.

Poem for Prerna

You look sheepish in your rainbow hat. You probably
wouldn't have mentioned the panic attacks if I hadn't
asked why you weren't on your trip to Kings Lynn.

I can't tell if you feel better or worse from them. Maybe
I never could.

How umbilical are we? Cut.

Sometimes I still need to reach out and stroke your back
to check you haven't become translucent.

Or more like lovers? Break-up.

Before you got back from the gym, wondering if I
should cook enough to share with you.

You say 'I love you' and I reply 'I know' and in a film that
would mean I don't love you.

How easy was it to be friends when I kept almost
making pop-corn for you to take to uni?

It cleaved us. You shivering electricity running through
your hands and feet jaw chattering.

Sometimes I look at you and taste the void beneath the
veneer on everything. It is so unmappable. I don't know
if I could live just two of us. We once planned for that, I
said I would take all our stuff in my car even though
I'm scared of driving.

We were never really planning to lodge in each other's
minds long term though anyway.

You found enough oxygen to ask me if I would ever
want to go to Syria with you and then to answer that
you already knew I wouldn't because I am too scared to
die. You were right, I have never felt the bodily urge to
face large-scale injustice.

I was already writing the scene of us – both on the
stairs, me looking up at you.

How easy is it to be friends if I say 'I can't be tangled up with you' when you say 'I love you'?

Sometimes I need to reach out and stroke your back to check I haven't become translucent.

Maybe if I made a huge vat of soup today and brought it to the picket line for everyone.

Between us

I will wash up for you before I leave
but, right now, the morning
can't bear too much activity. Drinking tea
is the warmth of holding and I need this
space between us. Everything is almost
on top of something else and your
birthday cake is not the only thing
that has lost its identity. A crisp packet
blossoms out of a wine glass. From here
I can almost see the whole of you. You are
probably okay, probably did not mind that I
showed up late, there were other people
to make you special and at least
I was there for the dancing. A moth flaps in
and I can feel you watching
her too. She brings echoes of you – *moths
are a quirk of this flat*, and me – *you should
seal your woollens in plastic.* I stand, clap quick.
She is dead in my palms. I am elated
like I've caught a ball impressively. I know you
will look away if I turn to you, won't want me
to be hurt by your shocked eyes. You know
I know anyway and so you feel
bad for hurting me. I could say sorry. I go
to the sink to wash her body away. She was
bigger and browner than most, she had
moved so slowly she'd made it look like
flight required all her concentration.

My Mum, 28th August 1962 – 26th July 2014
A Life Lived with the Strength
of a Warm Heart

Dad will brush back the leaves and hold his phone high above
while trying to keep his shoes out of shot. We will
laugh at him, *a wife's death*

is just so good for Facebook Likes. Then we'll all judge
the new epitaphs. 'Fall In Love but not In Line
and Remember it's Just a Ride' will be

hard to beat but our entry makes people feel
something un-domestic but also
cosy like mum made us

It's just the light

you are moths   that draws you to this death bed   my mum's

observe the timetable it took me so long to figure it all out   last light burning brighter

kethwump! kethwump!   please stop   please

do you want me to cry   let me

comfort you   death is so ubiquitous or she died ages ago when she stopped being

fat or we die every nanosecond according to buddhism or we live forever according to everyone or she's

my mother so maybe   she'll start screaming and the nurses won't listen

when i tell them to force feed the oxycodone so   please go she's wasted

the morning flirting with doctors   *you have to*   *they keep you alive*   and now she can't talk

please stay i don't know   what to do if she stops

my friends don't mention death because it's impolite   unbearably lonely

Iona are you too scared to let anyone love you? I was but I'm over it I don't need your help

to walk I'm as solid as a rock trust me we could make an escape

we say   A Life Lived with the Strength of a Warm Heart   please it's not true

that's what you'd say about a dead person   *I want to be buried in my pyjamas*

so it's cosy   i spoke to her on the phone   it was so nice but

i was pretending   i can feel her presence too or I think dad's

doing ok or please ask about me   i hate that   i'm fine   what a relief   she was so lucky

to die young   when all her friends could attend   to her beck and call

no you can't visit today we are all too weary and I know that means you probably won't see her again

Everything gets lost in the telling

When people ask about the hospital I do think about that moment with mum. Not the visuals of it but the feeling. Something like slight pressure underneath my face. Something like an ache in my throat and chest. But not much, 'a dull ache' haha. A not-quite-in-the-moment-ness an already-writing-the-poem-ness.

I never really thought she was dying but once I thought about living without her and Sally said I'd gone white and I thought 'my lips are white'.

But in the end I just tell them about those robot food carriers and the rumours that staff got sacked if they rode around on them.

Ankylosing Spondylitis

there's a super blue
blood red moon probably
actually on the other side

of my curtain but I'm not
going to check no I'm too
curled up the doctor said

my vertebrae are fusing
and it's not agony but it is
something constant and millions

of people are in their tidy rooms
peaking out at the night while I
become denser and bored of working out

what a happy person would do and then
doing it and now my house is a mess everyone
can see the insides of me anyway and maybe all my unspent

rage and tears and lust have crystallised
in my spine and when it's released it will be such a great spectacle
everyone will applaud or faint and I just want to be bothered to shatter

all those dirty mugs then smash up that table 'til walls can't contain me
and bits of brick and rooftiles crash down but feel just like breadcrumbs then
here is my super blue blood red body and there is the gaping sea and there
          are the miniscule streetlights

Watching the dancers

I want to be able to fly more than anything but
if I needed to work for it by doing things like jogging in the morning and
moisturising nightly would I bother? I can jump. In the moment before falling there's
all the people I don't see every day anymore and how little we touched and how often we
said how are you?   My waist is still so available. Anyone
could just rest their hand here and

Watching the puppets

So the trick is to pretend to need
the ground when really
it's the strings? If I let myself just
float. Then, would you still want to
look at me? Would I become
like a scarf on a hook?

A cat called Sadie

I woke up and didn't want to get up so started scrolling through RightMove even though that's the sort of thing that other people like to do and then when I was brushing my teeth I thought *I should live on a top floor flat all on my own and have a cat called Sadie*. I was so sure of the name Sadie that I can't have just come up with it. If I did name my cat Sadie I'd probably be copying someone without realising and they'd get offended. I'm not even sure what I think about cats, I mean I quite like them but I don't like saying how cute they are all the time. If I had my own flat then I'd have people round for dinner and they'd stroke Sadie with all their tender adoration and I'd have to say stuff like "awwwww look at her" and "would you like red or white wine". Whilst almost utterly engrossed by Sadie's long grey fur, my guest would remark "don't you think it's just so much easier with cats than with humans? A less complicated relationship". And what if I didn't just nod along and instead explained that it's not quite like that for me with cats but my heart does fill with delight for other things. Like a fruit bowl full of fruit or any body of water on a bright evening. They probably wouldn't make a fuss about it, say something like "oh yeah I'm sure it's exactly the same feeling" and that they'd have whatever colour wine I was having.

and the whole house

                               smells weird again, Richie says
it showed up this time last year and is in fact
a seasonal thing and he's probably right, makes me think –
could it be something to do with the heating? I should
do a thorough investigation round the radiators. Though
Elise pointed out that if a rat had died then it should've
done all its rotting by now. It's that sort of house,
you wouldn't be surprised to find a rat skeleton
between the fish tank and the microwave, well really
it's just a shared home with cluttered surfaces
we wipe them down more often than you might guess
and I love my housemates with a nonchalant certainty
you can't just get anywhere. Do you ever feel like
something is about to end but you don't know specifics?

Poem for Loïc's birthday

September is the kindest month – everything
effortless apples and blackberries. The pantry of your heart

so plentiful you can only just about imagine
the whisper of an empty echo.

And then the blessing of a sunny day that doesn't demand.
It could be

hot-chocolate on the bright doorstep
or cosy with a blanket and the soft dusk.

And you – Loïc – here in this pause, the whole world

your harvest. In years to come September will also bring
new shoes and stationery, the joyous rush

of friends after all that spaciousness. A chance
to reinvent yourself if you want to. It is possible

for worry to play amongst your eager hope but
beneath it all, a trust so deep that trees –

well, obviously – let go their dancing leaves and you
your palms to the sky. Lucky.

Could jump for joy

I'm in the garden with a woman a year younger than me holding the baby that will become me. Our apple tree is not there and she is so casual in the gap of its absence. Shocking. Even though I do know that is how time works.

Mum you look so effortlessly cool in that dress.

She must know I am her daughter from the future but she's not mentioning it because she doesn't want it to be awkward between us. I want to feel an easy friendship. I am jealous of the dress. I never want to feel ready to be a mum.

Is she thinking that too? She's not saying because she's worried I'd get sad. In that protectiveness we have already lost ourselves to each other.

Mum I could jump for joy if we could just have even one single moment before we get bound up so close and inevitable.

Everything here is so beautifully bright without those branches.

I am sorry apple tree, I did not intend to discover this.

ACKNOWLEDGEMENTS

I would like to thank the editors of the magazines, anthologies, and website in which some of these poems first appeared: 'Listen to this – ' was originally published in *Porridge Magazine*; 'What you do for mum's last Christmas' was originally published in the Dempsey and Windle anthology, *What the Peacock Replied*; 'Between us' was highly commended in the Sentinel Literary Quarterly poetry prize; 'It's just the light' was originally published in Poetry anthology for the 2017/18 MA in Creative Writing at UEA; 'Ankylosing Spondylitis' and 'Watching the puppets' were originally published by *Lighthouse Journal*.

A huge thank you to all the people who listened to me, laughed with me, and believed in me as I was writing this collection. Shout outs go to – Alice, Alvaro, Beth, Christina, Elise, Ellen, Em, Emma & Richard, Esme, Ethan, Fiona, Kate, Prerna, Richie, Snoozie, and you. Thank you also to the UEA 2017/2018 MA Poetry cohort and teachers.

An extra special mention to Dad and Sally, I love each of you so much.

I am grateful for my mum for all her love. And also for my goddessmother, Pat, for showing me how to be a dare-devil poet!

Finally, thank you to Rosey Priestman for illustrating the front cover with all your heart and to Stuart Bartholomew for choosing my poems, it is such an honour to be published by Verve Poetry Press!

ABOUT VERVE POETRY PRESS

Verve Poetry Press is a quite new and already award-winning press that focused initially on meeting a local need in Birmingham - a need for the vibrant poetry scene here in Brum to find a way to present itself to the poetry world via publication. Co-founded by Stuart Bartholomew and Amerah Saleh, it now publishes poets from all corners of the UK - poets that speak to the city's varied and energetic qualities and will contribute to its many poetic stories.

Added to this is a colourful pamphlet series, many featuring poets who have performed at our sister festival - and a poetry show series which captures the magic of longer poetry performance pieces by festival alumni such as Polarbear, Matt Abbott and Imogen Stirling.

The press has been voted Most Innovative Publisher at the Saboteur Awards, and has won the Publisher's Award for Poetry Pamphlets at the Michael Marks Awards.

Like the festival, we strive to think about poetry in inclusive ways and embrace the multiplicity of approaches towards this glorious art.

www.vervepoetrypress.com
@VervePoetryPres
mail@vervepoetrypress.com